JR/pn p.17 textures metal/th
B/T 18
18   ds
19 Classification BKS.
Animals - farm
Jr. p.15 Folders,   seed   zoo pets
p.?,6 Boards   fat,veg,mt water
seasons
p.10 Pres. - Cubes (seq)   vehicles   homes
land,sea,air of animals

Teaching
Toys

dark & Lt
p.28 Jr./Pres. Colorwheel & clothespin
textures, patters

Jr. p.38 donut/snake match - patterns
40   textures

By Jean Warren

Illustrated by Paula Inmon

pres. 44 Category cards: shapes, animals
Jr. 50 pocket sort
travel - cake pan = magnet bd
p.32 class - cooky sheet
geometric shapes to make pict.
Jr. p.58 dif. shapes sizes colors △   + patterns
p.35 pres. FB - picts "Continuous story
way
- seq: picts (baby → old man)
- size
- spatial concepts in/out

fish - colors   starfset - block   buttons - eat. patterns
22 size   24 Cork   sort
shapes   sponge
cut.   gum erasers
Totline happy/sad   cooky cutters

Warren Publishing House, Inc.
P.O. Box 2255, Everett, WA 98203

decals p.4 - stickers

Editor: Elizabeth S. McKinnon
Contributing Editor: Sue Foster
Production Editors: Gayle Bittinger
                     Claudia G. Reid
Cover Design: Larry Countryman

ISBN 0-911019-16-2

Library of Congress Catalog Card Number 87-050757
Printed in the United States of America

Contents

Introduction

Let's face it — teaching comes alive when we can develop our own learning materials. So at Totline we have put together this book of 28 multi-usuable teaching aids, each of which can be made easily and inexpensively and fashioned to teach a variety of learning concepts.

On the following pages you will find suggestions for making over 100 toys and games to teach colors, numbers, basic shapes, alphabet letters, beginning sounds — and more. By using these suggestions as starting points, you can create any number of original and unique learning materials that are especially suited for your children.

Discover the possibilities!

Jean Warren

Teaching Placemats

Materials: Large sheets of construction paper; ruler; felt-tip markers; clear Con-Tact paper; index cards; crayons; game markers (dried beans, raisins, Cheerios, etc.); patterned wrapping paper; pair of scissors; tagboard; tape.

General Directions: Make gameboards on large sheets of construction paper and cover them with clear Con-Tact paper. Then use the gameboards as placemats and let the children play games on them before snack time.

Color Placemats — Divide large sheets of construction paper into six or more squares each and draw different colored circles in the squares. Draw matching colored circles on index cards. As you hold up a card, have the children use crayons to X-out the matching colored circles on their gameboards. When the game is over, wipe the gameboards with a damp paper towel to remove the crayon.

Number Placemats — Divide large sheets of construction paper into six or more squares each and write different numerals in the upper left-hand corners of the squares. Set out a large bowl of dried beans, raisins, etc., to use as markers. Then let the children place corresponding numbers of markers in the squares on their gameboards.

Shape Placemats — Make a gameboard for each group of two or three children. In the upper left-hand corner of a large piece of construction paper, draw a circle and write "Start" inside of it. Then draw a pathway of geometric shapes (circles, squares, triangles, etc.), in random order, winding around the

6

paper. End with a circle in the lower right-hand corner marked "Finish." Make three or four game cards for each shape by drawing the shapes on index cards. Put the deck of cards face down and give each child a different kind of game marker to place on the "Start" circle. As each child turns up a card, have the child move his or her marker to the next shape designated by the card.

Picture Placemats — To make each gameboard, cover a large rectangle of wrapping paper that contains a pattern of pictures with clear Con-Tact paper. From a matching sheet of wrapping paper, cut out five or six of the pictures and cover them with clear Con-Tact paper also. Tape squares of tagboard on the backs of the gameboards to make envelopes for holding the cutouts. Then let the children match the pictures by placing the cutouts on top of the corresponding pictures on the gameboards.

Other Suggestions: For more gameboard ideas, see Teaching Folders on p. 14 and Teaching Lotto on p. 16.

Teaching Placemats

7

Teaching Crowns

Materials: Assorted colors of construction paper (large and small sheets); pair of scissors; magazines; glue; felt-tip marker; assorted kinds of small items (buttons, stickers, paper clips, etc.); assorted kinds of textured materials (velvet, burlap, sandpaper, etc.); tape.

General Directions: Cut crown shapes out of large sheets of construction paper. Have the children glue pictures, shapes, etc., on their crowns. Then tape the ends of each crown together in the back.

Color Crowns — Choose a color such as red and make crowns out of red construction paper. Let the children look through magazines to find red pictures. Then have them tear out the pictures and glue them on their crowns. (Let younger children choose from precut pictures that have been placed in a box.)

Number Crowns — On the front of each crown, write a numeral such as "3." Then let the children glue different sets of three items (three buttons, three stickers, etc.) on their crowns.

Shape Crowns — Choose a geometric shape such as a triangle. Cut various colors and sizes of triangles out of construction paper and let the children glue them on their crowns.

Crown for a day (ie # day, animal)

Texture Crowns — Cut different kinds of textured materials into small pieces. Then let the children glue combinations of rough and smooth textured materials on their crowns.

Holiday Crowns — Choose appropriate colored construction paper to make crowns and shapes for each holiday (red and pink for Valentine's Day, orange and black for Halloween, etc.). Cut out holiday shapes (hearts, pumpkins, etc.) in a variety of sizes and let the children glue them on their crowns.

Other Suggestions: Use magazine pictures to make animal crowns, food crowns, transportation crowns, etc.; use actual items to make leaf crowns, shell crowns, seed crowns, etc.

Teaching Crowns

Teaching Cubes

Materials: Clear plastic photo cubes; large index cards; pair of scissors; felt-tip markers; construction paper; tape.

General Directions: Cut index cards to fit in the sides of the photo cubes. Draw pictures, shapes, etc., on the cards and insert them in the cubes. Then let the children use the cubes to play various kinds of learning games.

Color Cubes — Put different colored cards in the sides of one photo cube. Put matching colored cards in the sides of another photo cube in a different order. Then let the children move the cubes around to find the matching pairs of colors.

Number Cubes — Put cards containing different numerals in the sides of one photo cube. Put cards containing corresponding numbers of dots or small pictures in the sides of another photo cube in a different order. Then let the children move the cubes around to find the matching pairs of numbers.

Shape Cubes — Put cards containing different basic shapes (a circle, a square, a triangle, a star, etc.) in the sides of one photo cube. Put cards containing matching shapes in the sides of another photo cube in a different order. Then let the children move the cubes around to find the matching pairs of shapes.

Sequence Cubes — Put cards containing pictures that illustrate a sequence in the sides of three or four photo cubes (a seed in the ground, a sprout, a flower in bloom; a tree in spring, a tree in summer, a tree in fall, a tree in winter; etc.). Then let the children line up the photo cubes in the proper sequence.

10

Dice Cubes — Let the children use a Number Cube as a die when playing games. For example, tape construction paper circles to the floor to make "stepping stones" for a start-to-finish game. Let the children take turns rolling the die, naming the number that comes up and then taking that number of steps toward the finish line.

Other Suggestions: Match capital letters with corresponding lower case letters; match alphabet letters with pictures of things whose names begin with those letters; match pictures of animals, foods, vehicles, etc.

Teaching Cubes

Teaching Windows

Materials: A large sheet of tagboard; clear plastic photo holders; tape; metal paper fasteners; large index cards; pair of scissors; felt-tip markers; yarn.

General Directions: Tape a row of clear plastic photo holders down each side of a large sheet of tagboard. Attach a metal paper fastener next to each photo holder toward the center of the board. Cut index cards to fit inside the photo holders. Draw pictures, shapes, etc., on one set of cards and insert them in the photo holders in the left-hand row. Make a matching set of cards and insert them in the photo holders in the right-hand row in a different order. Tie short pieces of yarn to the paper fasteners on the left. Then let the children match the cards by winding the loose ends of the yarn pieces around the appropriate paper fasteners on the right. Change the cards in the photo holders each day to reinforce a different learning concept.

Color Windows — Put different colored cards in the photo holders on the left. Put matching colored cards or cards containing matching colored pictures in the photo holders on the right.

Number Windows — Put cards containing different numerals in the photo holders on the left. Put cards containing corresponding numbers of dots or small pictures in the photo holders on the right.

Shape Windows — Put cards containing different geometric shapes (a circle, a square, a triangle, etc.) in the photo holders on the left. Put cards containing matching geometric shapes or shape pictures (a ball, a box, a clown hat, etc.) in the photo holders on the right.

Beginning Sounds Windows — Put cards containing different alphabet letters in the photo holders on the left. Put cards containing pictures of things whose names begin with those letters in the photo holders on the right.

Animal Windows — Put cards containing pictures of different animal mothers in the photo holders on the left. Put cards containing pictures of corresponding animal babies or animal homes in the photo holders on the right.

Other Suggestions: Match capital letters with lower case letters; match squares of patterned wallpaper or wrapping paper; match pictures of holiday shapes, foods, articles of clothing, etc.

Teaching Windows

Teaching Folders

Materials: File folders; felt-tip markers; clear Con-Tact paper; tagboard or large index cards; pair of scissors; tape.

General Directions: Draw pictures on the insides of file folders to make gameboards and cover them with clear Con-Tact paper. Make game cards by drawing matching pictures on tagboard or index cards, covering them with clear Con-Tact paper and then cutting them out. Tape squares of tagboard on the fronts of the file folders to make envelopes for holding the game cards. Then let the children use the folders to play matching and sorting games.

Color Folders — Draw eight different colored bears, stars, etc., on the insides of each file folder. Draw matching colored pictures on tagboard and cut them out. Then let the children match the colors by placing the cutouts on top of the corresponding pictures on the file folders.

Number Folders — Draw eight apples, suns, etc., on the insides of each file folder and write a different numeral inside each picture. Draw matching pictures that contain corresponding numbers of dots on tagboard and cut them out. Then let the children match the numbers by placing the cutouts on top of the corresponding pictures on the file folders.

Shape Folders — Draw eight basic shapes (a circle, a square, a triangle, a star, etc.) on the insides of each file folder. Draw matching shapes on tagboard and cut them out. Then let the children match the shapes by placing the cutouts on top of the corresponding shapes on the file folders.

Alphabet Folders — Draw eight flowers, hearts, etc., on the insides of each file folder and write a different capital letter inside each picture. Draw matching pictures that contain corresponding lower case letters on tagboard and cut them out. Then let the children match the letters by placing the cutouts on top of the corresponding pictures on the file folders.

Classification Folders — Choose a subject such as animals and label one side of an open file folder "Farm" and the other side "Zoo" (or draw pictures to indicate the labels.) Draw pictures of farm animals and zoo animals on tagboard and cut them out. Then let the children sort the pictures by placing them on the appropriate sides of the file folder.

Other Suggestions: Match picture stickers; match pictures cut from canned goods labels, magazine ads, etc. Sort pictures of shapes (circles-squares, etc.); sort pictures of foods (fruits-vegetables, etc.).

Teaching Folders

Teaching Lotto

Materials: Tagboard; ruler; felt-tip markers; pair of scissors; assorted colors of construction paper; glue; tape.

General Directions: Cut tagboard into 9-inch squares to make gameboards. Divide each gameboard into nine squares and draw pictures, shapes, etc., in the squares. For each gameboard, make a set of nine matching game cards on 3-inch squares cut from tagboard. Tape large squares of tagboard on the backs of the gameboards to make envelopes for holding the game cards. Then let the children play matching games by placing the game cards on top of the corresponding squares on the gameboards.

Color Lotto — For each gameboard, cut nine 3-inch squares out of different colors of construction paper and glue the squares on the gameboard. Cut matching 3-inch squares out of construction paper and glue them on the nine game cards.

Number Lotto — On each gameboard, draw a different number of small pictures in each square (three balloons in one square, five flowers in another square, etc.). Write corresponding numerals on the nine game cards.

Shape Lotto — On each gameboard, draw a different basic shape (a circle, a square, a triangle, a star, etc.) in each square. Draw matching shapes on the nine game cards.

Alphabet Lotto — On each gameboard, write a different capital letter in each square. Write corresponding lower case letters on the nine game cards.

Beginning Sounds Lotto — On each gameboard, draw a picture of something whose name begins with a different sound in each square (a bee in one square, a fork in another square, etc.). Write the corresponding beginning alphabet letters on the nine game cards.

Other Suggestions: Match pictures of animals, foods, vehicles, etc.; match squares of patterned wallpaper or wrapping paper; match squares of textured materials (velvet, burlap, sandpaper, etc.).

Teaching Lotto

Teaching Books

Materials: White construction paper or typing paper; colored construction paper; stapler; felt-tip markers; magazines and catalogs; glue.

General Directions: Make a book for each child by stapling four sheets of white paper together with a colored construction paper cover. Title the cover according to a selected learning concept ("Red Book," "Number Book," etc.). Let the children look through magazines and catalogs to find pictures that illustrate the learning concept. Then have them tear out the pictures and glue them in their books. (Let younger children choose from precut pictures that have been placed in a box.)

Color Books — Choose a color such as red and make book covers out of red construction paper. Then have the children glue pictures of red things throughout their books. Or label the pages of the books with different colors and let the children glue on corresponding colored pictures.

Number Books — Number the pages of each book from 1 to 8. Then have the children glue pictures of one thing, pictures of two things, etc., on the corresponding numbered pages in their books.

Shape Books — Choose a geometric shape such as a circle and have the children glue pictures of circular things throughout their books. Or label the pages of the books with different geometric shapes (circles, squares, triangles, etc.) and have the children glue on corresponding shaped pictures.

Beginning Sounds Books — Label the pages of the books with different alphabet letters. Then have the children glue pictures of things whose names begin with those letters on the appropriate pages in their books.

Classification Books — Choose a subject such as foods and label the book pages "Breakfast," "Lunch" and "Dinner." Then have the children glue pictures of foods they usually eat for those meals on the appropriate pages in their books.

Other Suggestions: Make animal books, toy books, pet books, etc. Use textured materials (velvet, burlap, sandpaper, etc.) to make texture books; use nature items (leaves, flowers, seeds, etc.) to make nature books.

Teaching Books

Teaching Sticks

Materials: A large shoebox; knife; tongue depressors; assorted colors and kinds of stickers (self-stick dots, picture stickers, shapes cut from scraps of colored Con-Tact paper, etc.); felt-tip marker.

General Directions: Turn the shoebox upside down and cut two parallel rows of slits in the top. Decorate the ends of one set of tongue depressors with shape stickers, alphabet letters, etc. Decorate the ends of another set of tongue depressors to match. Insert one set of tongue depressors in one of the rows of slits. Then let the children insert matching tongue depressors from the second set in the appropriate slits in the other row.

Color Sticks — Attach different colored stickers to one set of tongue depressors and matching colored stickers to another set.

Number Sticks — Write different numerals on one set of tongue depressors and attach corresponding numbers of stickers to another set.

Shape Sticks — Attach stickers cut into different basic shapes (a circle, a square, a triangle, a star, etc.) to one set of tongue depressors and matching shaped stickers to another set.

Alphabet Sticks — Write different capital letters on one set of tongue depressors and corresponding lower case letters on another set.

Picture Sticks — Attach different picture stickers to one set of tongue depressors and matching picture stickers to another set.

Other Suggestions: Make sticks for sorting colors (red in one row, blue in the other row, etc.); make sticks for sorting shapes (circles in one row, squares in the other row, etc.). Use unmarked tongue depressors for playing counting games.

Teaching Sticks

Teaching Fish

Materials: A fishing pole (3 feet of string tied to a paper towel tube, a wooden spoon, etc.); small magnet; assorted colors of construction paper; pair of scissors; felt-tip markers; paper clips.

General Directions: Tie a magnet to the end of the string on the fishing pole. Cut fish shapes out of construction paper and attach a paper clip to each fish. Then lay the shapes out on the floor and let the children take turns "catching fish" as you give directions.

Color Fish — Cut fish shapes out of different colors of construction paper. Ask the children to catch just the red fish, just the yellow fish, etc.

Number Fish — Ask the children to catch five fish, three fish, etc. Or write numerals on the fish shapes and ask the children to catch a "two" fish, a "four" fish, etc.

Shape Fish — Cut geometric shapes (circles, squares, triangles, etc.) out of construction paper. Ask the children to catch just the circles, just the triangles, etc.

Size Fish — Cut out various sizes of fish shapes. Ask each child in turn to catch the largest fish, then the smallest. When all the fish have been caught, let the children sort them into piles of small fish, medium-sized fish and large fish.

fish — color
size
shapes

Beginning Sounds Fish — Choose a sound such as the "h" sound. On fish shapes, draw pictures of things whose names begin with that sound (a house, a hat, etc.). On several other fish shapes, draw pictures of things whose names begin with different sounds (a pig, a car, etc.). As the fish are caught, ask the children to name the pictures and tell whether or not the names begin with the chosen sound.

Other Suggestions: Write alphabet letters on fish shapes and catch "A" fish, "D" fish, etc. Draw different kinds of faces on fish shapes and catch happy fish, sad fish, sleepy fish, etc.

Teaching Fish

Teaching Stamps

Materials: White construction paper; assorted materials for making stamps (potato halves, sponges, gum erasers, corks, etc.); assorted items to use as stamps (cookie cutters, small wooden blocks, jar lids, etc.); knife; pair of scissors; tempera paints; Styrofoam meat trays; paper towels; felt-tip marker.

General Directions: Carve or cut a variety of stamping materials into different shapes (stars, flowers, squares, etc.). Make paint pads by placing folded paper towels in meat trays and pouring on paints. Set out the carved stamps along with cookie cutters, wooden blocks, etc. Then let the children dip the stamps into the paint and press them on their papers to make prints.

Color Stamps — Choose a color such as red and prepare red paint pads. Then let the children use a variety of stamps to print red shapes on their papers.

Number Stamps — At the top of each paper, write a numeral such as "3." Then let the children use a variety of stamps to print different sets of three shapes (three diamonds, three fish, etc.) on their papers.

Shape Stamps — Choose a geometric shape such as a circle and cut a variety of stamping materials into circle shapes. Then let the children use the stamps along with jar lids, spools, etc., to print circle shapes on their papers.

Pattern Stamps — Use stamps to start patterns for the children to continue printing down the lengths of their papers (red, blue, red, blue; circle, square, triangle, circle, square, triangle; etc.).

Holiday Stamps — Choose a holiday shape such as a heart and cut a variety of stamping materials into heart shapes. Then let the children use the stamps along with heart shaped cookie cutters to print red and pink hearts on their papers.

Other Suggestions: Match color prints; match shape prints. Classify colors (red prints on one side of the paper, blue prints on the other side, etc.); classify shapes (circle prints on one side of the paper, square prints on the other side, etc.).

Teaching Stamps

Teaching Clothesline

Materials: A length of clothesline or heavy cord; two chairs; clothespins; assorted colors of fabric; pair of scissors; basket.

General Directions: Hang a length of clothesline between two chairs and clip clothespins on the line. Cut clothing shapes (shirts, pants, socks, etc.) out of fabric and place them in a basket. Then let the children take turns "hanging up the wash" as you give directions.

Color Clothesline — Cut clothing shapes out of different colors of fabric. Ask the children to hang up just the green clothes, just the yellow clothes, etc. Or hang different colored clothing shapes on the line and ask the children to hang matching colored shapes next to them.

Number Clothesline — Ask the children to hang up five clothing shapes, three clothing shapes, etc. Or ask them to hang up two shirts and one dress, etc., and then tell how many shapes there are all together.

Shape Clothesline — Cut geometric shapes (circles, squares, triangles, etc.) out of fabric. Ask the children to hang up just the triangles, just the circles, etc. Or hang different geometric shapes on the line and ask the children to hang matching shapes next to them.

Clothing Clothesline — Ask the children to hang up just the socks, just the dresses, etc. Or ask them to hang the pants on one side of the line and the shirts on the other side, etc.

Pattern Clothesline — Ask the children to hang up the wash in patterns (red, blue, red, blue; circle, square, circle, square; pants, shirt, sock, pants, shirt, sock; etc.).

Other Suggestions: Hang up pairs of clothing shapes cut from matching patterned fabric (striped, checked, flowered, etc.); hang up pairs of clothing shapes cut from matching textured fabric (velvet, satin, corduroy, etc.).

Teaching Clothesline

Teaching Wheel

Materials: Tagboard; pair of scissors; ruler; felt-tip markers; spring-type clothespins.

General Directions: Cut a 12-inch circle out of tagboard. Divide the circle into eight sections and draw shapes, alphabet letters, etc., in the sections. Draw matching shapes, letters, etc., on eight clothespins. Then let the children clip the clothespins around the edge of the wheel on the matching sections.

Color Wheel — Color each section of the wheel a different color. Color eight clothespins to match. *dark + lt. colors*

Number Wheel — Draw a different number of dots or small pictures in each section of the wheel. Write corresponding numerals on eight clothespins.

Shape Wheel — Draw a different basic shape (a circle, a square, a triangle, a star, etc.) in each section of the wheel. Draw matching shapes on eight clothespins.

Alphabet Wheel — Write a different capital letter in each section of the wheel. Write corresponding lower case letters on eight clothespins.

Beginning Sounds Wheel — Draw a picture of something whose name begins with a different sound in each section of the wheel (a balloon in one section, a leaf in another section, etc.). Write the corresponding beginning alphabet letters on eight clothespins.

Other Suggestions: Match pieces of textured materials (velvet, burlap, sandpaper, etc.); match pieces of patterned wallpaper or wrapping paper.

Teaching Wheel

Teaching Clips

Materials: Tongue depressors; spring-type clothespins; strong glue; small index cards; felt-tip markers; pair of scissors.

General Directions: Make a set of clips by gluing two clothespins (2½ inches apart) on a tongue depressor so that the clip ends of the clothespins are hanging down. To make each pair of game cards, fold a small index card in half and draw matching shapes, alphabet letters, etc., on the two halves. Draw a small star in the upper left-hand corner of the index card and another small star in the upper right-hand corner. Turn the card over and draw a large shape (any kind) in the center of the back. Then cut the card in half along the fold. Follow the same procedure to make a set of matching cards for each selected learning concept. To play, have the children clip matching cards to the clothespins with the stars in the upper left- and upper right-hand corners. If the matches are correct, the shapes drawn on the backs of the cards will fit together like puzzles.

Color Clips — Draw a different colored circle on one half of each index card and a matching colored circle on the other half. Or write a different color word ("Red," "Blue," etc.) on one half of each index card and draw a matching colored circle on the other half.

Number Clips — Write a different numeral on one half of each index card and draw a corresponding number of dots or small pictures on the other half.

Shape Clips — Draw a different geometric shape (a circle, a square, a triangle, etc.) on one half of each index card and a matching geometric shape or shape picture (a ball, a box, a clown hat, etc.) on the other half.

Alphabet Clips — Write a different capital letter on one half of each index card and a corresponding lower case letter on the other half.

Beginning Sounds Clips — Write a different alphabet letter on one half of each index card and draw a picture of something whose name begins with that letter on the other half.

Other Suggestions: Match squares of patterned wallpaper or wrapping paper; match pieces of textured materials (velvet, burlap, sandpaper, etc.); match picture stickers; match pictures of animals, foods, articles of clothing, etc.

Teaching Clips

Teaching Magnetboard

cake pan

Materials: A magnetboard (a cookie sheet, a pizza pan, a refrigerator door, etc.); assorted colors of tagboard; pair of scissors; small magnets or magnetic tape (available at hardware stores); glue; felt-tip marker.

General Directions: Cut shapes out of tagboard. Attach small magnets or strips of magnetic tape to the backs of the shapes. Then let the children place the shapes on the magnetboard as you give directions. (Note: Shapes can also be made out of playdough and backed with small magnets.)

Color Magnetboard — Cut shapes (bears, stars, etc.) out of different colors of tagboard. Ask the children to place just the red shapes on the magnetboard, just the blue shapes, etc. Or place different colored shapes on the magnetboard and ask the children to place matching colored shapes next to them.

Number Magnetboard — Cut five squares out of tagboard and number them from 1 to 5. Ask the children to line up the numerals on the magnetboard in the proper sequence. Or place sets of shapes (two suns, five hearts, etc.) on the magnetboard and ask the children to place corresponding numerals next to them.

Shape Magnetboard — Cut geometric shapes (circles, squares, triangles, etc.) out of tagboard. Ask the children to place just the squares on the magnetboard, just the triangles, etc. Or place different geometric shapes on the magnetboard and ask the children to place matching geometric shapes next to them.

Alphabet Magnetboard — Cut squares out of tagboard. Write capital letters on one set of squares and corresponding lower case letters on another set. Place the capital letters on the magnetboard and ask the children to place the corresponding lower case letters next to them. (Older children can use the letters to spell words.)

Picture Magnetboard — Cut various sizes of geometric shapes out of tagboard. Then let the children put the shapes together on the magnetboard to create pictures of people, houses, robots, etc.

Other Suggestions: Use shapes to make math equations (two stars plus three circles, etc.); use shapes to make patterns (red, blue, red, blue; circle, square, triangle, circle, square, triangle; etc.).

Teaching Magnetboard

Teaching Flannelboard

Materials: A large piece of plywood or heavy cardboard; large piece of flannel material; tape or stapler; pair of scissors; assorted colors of felt; magazines or old books; glue.

General Directions: Cover a large sheet of plywood or heavy cardboard with flannel. Tape or staple the edges of the flannel to the back of the board. Cut felt into shapes, numerals, etc. Cut pictures out of magazines or old books and back them with felt strips. Then let the children place the cutouts on the flannelboard as you give directions. (Note: Small carpet squares can be used for individual flannelboards.)

Color Flannelboard — Cut shapes (fish, hearts, etc.) out of different colors of felt. Ask the children to place just the yellow shapes on the flannelboard, just the red shapes, etc. Or place different colored shapes on the flannelboard and ask the children to place matching colored shapes next to them.

Number Flannelboard — Cut the numerals 1 to 5 out of felt. Ask the children to line up the numerals on the flannelboard in the proper sequence. Or place sets of shapes (three stars, two diamonds, etc.) on the flannelboard and ask the children to place corresponding numerals next to them.

Shape Flannelboard — Cut geometric shapes (circles, squares, triangles, etc.) out of felt. Ask the children to place just the circles on the flannelboard, just the squares, etc. Or place different geometric shapes on the flannelboard and ask the children to place matching geometric shapes next to them.

Beginning Sounds Flannelboard — Cut an alphabet letter such as "B" out of felt and place it on the flannelboard. Cut out pictures of things whose names begin with the "b" sound (a balloon, a ball, etc.) along with several pictures of things whose names begin with other sounds (a cat, a tree, etc.). Then ask the children to sort through the pictures and place those whose names begin with the "b" sound on the flannelboard.

Language Flannelboard — Cut pictures out of magazines or old books. Place the pictures on the flannelboard one at a time and let the children use them to make up a continuous story. Or let each child choose a picture, place it on the flannelboard and tell a few sentences about it.

Other Suggestions: Line up pictures that illustrate a sequence (a baby, a child, an adult; etc.). Classify shapes or pictures by size (big and little). Place shapes or pictures on the flannelboard to reinforce concepts of over and under, top, bottom and middle, etc.

Teaching Flannelboard

Teaching Pegboard

Materials: A large piece of pegboard; peg hooks; small index cards; pair of scissors; felt-tip markers; clear Con-Tact paper; hole punch.

General Directions: Hang peg hooks down the pegboard in two parallel rows. Cut index cards in half. Draw shapes, alphabet letters, etc., on one set of cards and make another set of cards to match. Cover the cards with clear Con-Tact paper and punch a hole in the top of each card. Hang one set of cards on the peg hooks in the left-hand row. Then let the children hang matching cards from the second set on the appropriate peg hooks in the right-hand row. (Note: A wooden board with cup hooks screwed into it can be substituted for the pegboard and peg hooks.)

Color Pegboard — Draw different colored circles on one set of cards and matching colored circles on another set. Or draw different colored pictures on one set of cards and matching colored circles on another set.

Number Pegboard — Write different numerals on one set of cards and draw corresponding numbers of dots or small pictures on another set.

Shape Pegboard — Draw different geometric shapes (a circle, a square, a triangle, etc.) on one set of cards and matching geometric shapes or shape pictures (a ball, a box, a clown hat, etc.) on another set.

Alphabet Pegboard — Write different capital letters on one set of cards and corresponding lower case letters on another set.

Beginning Sounds Pegboard — Write different alphabet letters on one set of cards and draw pictures of things whose names begin with those letters on another set.

Other Suggestions: Match picture stickers; match pictures cut from canned goods labels, magazine ads, etc.; match patterned squares of wallpaper or wrapping paper; match pictures of animal mothers and animal babies, animals and animal homes, etc.

Teaching Pegboard

Teaching Donuts

Materials: A large sheet of tagboard; pair of scissors; ruler; felt-tip marker; assorted colors and kinds of stickers (self-stick dots, picture stickers, shapes cut from scraps of colored Con-Tact paper, etc.).

General Directions: Cut an 18-inch circle out of tagboard. Go in 3 inches from the edge and cut out a smaller circle. Then go in 3 inches from the edge of the smaller circle and cut out a third circle. You will end up with two donuts and a small circle "pie," each of which can be made into a separate matching game. Use a felt-tip marker to divide the large donut into ten sections, the small donut into six sections and the pie into four sections. On opposite sides of each dividing line, attach matching stickers or write corresponding alphabet letters, etc. Cut out the sections and place them in three separate Ziploc bags. Then let the children piece together the donuts and the pie by matching the stickers, letters, etc., on the ends of the sections.

Color Donuts — Attach a different colored sticker on one side of each dividing line and a matching colored sticker on the other side.

Number Donuts — Write a different numeral on one side of each dividing line and attach a corresponding number of stickers on the other side.

Shape Donuts — Attach a sticker cut into a different basic shape (a circle, a square, a triangle, a star, etc.) on one side of each dividing line and a matching shaped sticker on the other side.

Alphabet Donuts — Write a different capital letter on one side of each dividing line and a corresponding lower case letter on the other side.

Picture Donuts — Attach a different picture sticker on one side of each dividing line and a matching picture sticker on the other side.

Other Suggestions: For more matching ideas, see Teaching Worm on p. 40.

Teaching Donuts

39

Teaching Worm

Materials: A large sheet of construction paper; pair of scissors; felt-tip markers; clear Con-Tact paper; assorted kinds of textured materials (velvet, burlap, sandpaper, etc.); glue.

General Directions: Cut a large, rounded worm shape out of construction paper. Use a felt-tip marker to draw on facial features and to divide the worm into six or more sections. On opposite sides of each dividing line, draw matching shapes, patterns, etc. Cover the worm shape with clear Con-Tact paper and cut out the sections. Then let the children piece the worm together by matching the shapes, patterns, etc., on the ends of the sections.

Color Worm — Color the area on one side of each dividing line a different color and the area on the other side a matching color.

Number Worm — Write a different numeral on one side of each dividing line and draw a corresponding number of dots or small pictures on the other side.

Shape Worm — Draw a different basic shape (a circle, a square, a triangle, a star, etc.) on one side of each dividing line and a matching shape on the other side.

Pattern Worm — Draw a different pattern (stripes, squiggles, etc.) in the area on one side of each dividing line and a matching pattern in the area on the other side.

Texture Worm — Glue a piece of different textured material on one half of each dividing line and a piece of matching textured material on the other side. (Cover just the back of the worm shape with clear Con-Tact paper.)

Other Suggestions: Match capital letters with lower case letters; match alphabet letters with pictures of things whose names begin with those letters; match picture stickers.

Teaching Worm

Teaching Dominoes

Materials: Tagboard or small index cards; ruler; pair of scissors; felt-tip markers; picture stickers.

General Directions: Cut tagboard or index cards into 21 small cards (about 1½ by 4 inches each). Divide each card in half with a line and draw a shape, a set of dots, etc., in each half. Give each child a number of cards and place the remaining cards face down in a pile. Let one child begin by placing a card in the middle of the playing area. If the next child has a card with a half that matches one of the halves of the first card, have the child place the card next to the first card so that the matching halves are touching (either vertically or horizontally). If the child does not have a matching card, let him or her draw cards from the pile until a match is found. Continue the game, letting the children match the cards any way they wish, until all the cards have been played.

Color Dominoes — Choose six colors such as red, yellow, blue, green, orange and purple. Draw two colored circles on each of the 21 cards, using these combinations: red-red, red-yellow, red-blue, red-green, red-orange, red-purple; yellow-yellow, yellow-blue, yellow-green, yellow-orange, yellow-purple; blue-blue, blue-green, blue-orange, blue-purple; green-green, green-orange, green-purple; orange-orange, orange-purple; purple-purple.

Number Dominoes — Choose six numbers such as 0, 1, 2, 3, 4 and 5. Draw two sets of dots to represent the numbers on each of the 21 cards (for 0, leave the cards blank). Use these combinations: 0-0, 0-1, 0-2, 0-3, 0-4, 0-5; 1-1, 1-2, 1-3, 1-4, 1-5; 2-2, 2-3, 2-4, 2-5; 3-3, 3-4, 3-5; 4-4, 4-5; 5-5.

Shape Dominoes — Choose six basic shapes such as a circle, a square, a triangle, a rectangle, a diamond and a star. Draw two shapes on each of the 21 cards, using these combinations: circle-circle, circle-square, circle-triangle, circle-rectangle, circle-diamond, circle-star; square-square, square-triangle, square-rectangle, square-diamond, square-star; triangle-triangle, triangle-rectangle, triangle-diamond, triangle-star; rectangle-rectangle, rectangle-diamond, rectangle-star; diamond-diamond, diamond-star; star-star.

Picture Dominoes — Choose six different picture stickers such as a bear, a flower, a cat, a rainbow, a duck and a clown (7 of each). Attach two stickers on each of the 21 cards, using these combinations: bear-bear, bear-flower, bear-cat, bear-rainbow, bear-duck, bear-clown; flower-flower, flower-cat, flower-rainbow, flower-duck, flower-clown; cat-cat, cat-rainbow, cat-duck, cat-clown; rainbow-rainbow, rainbow-duck, rainbow-clown; duck-duck, duck-clown; clown-clown.

Teaching Dominoes

43

Teaching Mailboxes

Materials: Shoeboxes with lids; construction paper; pair of scissors; tape; knife; felt-tip markers; small index cards; envelopes.

General Directions: Make mailboxes by covering the lids of three or more shoeboxes with construction paper and cutting a slit in the top of each lid. Put the lids on the boxes. Draw shapes, alphabet letters, etc., on small index cards and tape them to the backs of the mailboxes so that they stand above the lids. Make "letters" for the mailboxes by drawing matching shapes, alphabet letters, etc., on the fronts of sealed envelopes. Then mix up the letters and let the children take turns "mailing" them through the slots of the appropriate mailboxes.

Color Mailboxes — Tape different colored cards to the backs of the mailboxes. Draw matching colored circles or pictures on the fronts of the envelopes.

Number Mailboxes — Tape cards containing different numerals to the backs of the mailboxes. Draw corresponding numbers of dots or small pictures on the fronts of the envelopes.

Shape Mailboxes — Tape cards containing different basic shapes (a circle, a square, a triangle, a star, etc.) to the backs of the mailboxes. Draw matching shapes on the fronts of the envelopes.

Alphabet Mailboxes — Tape cards containing different capital letters to the backs of the mailboxes. Write corresponding lower case letters on the fronts of the envelopes.

Feelings Mailboxes — Tape cards containing different faces (happy, sad, sleepy, etc.) to the backs of the mailboxes. Draw matching faces on the fronts of the envelopes.

Other Suggestions: Match alphabet letters with pictures of things whose names begin with those letters; match pictures of animals, foods, articles of clothing, etc.

Teaching Mailboxes

Teaching Graph

Materials: A large sheet of tagboard; ruler; clear Con-Tact paper; felt-tip markers (water-based).

General Directions: On a large sheet of tagboard, draw lines to make an outline for a bar graph. Write the numerals 1 to 12 across the top of the outline. Cover the tagboard with clear Con-Tact paper. Then use the graph outline each day to record the results of a survey you take with the children. Choose a topic such as birthdays. Title the graph "Our Birthdays" and list the categories "Spring," "Summer," "Fall" and "Winter" (or draw pictures to indicate the categories). Count with the children how many of them have birthdays in spring, how many have birthdays in summer, etc. Then record the numbers by drawing bars on the graph. Discuss the results of the survey. Ask questions such as "Which group is smaller, the one with birthdays in summer or the one with birthdays in winter? How many more have birthdays in spring than have birthdays in fall?" When you have finished, wipe the graph with a damp paper towel to remove the marker ink.

Color Graph — Title the graph "Our Shirts" and list categories such as "White," "Blue," "Green" and "Yellow." Have the children count how many of them are wearing white shirts, how many are wearing blue shirts, etc.

Number Graph — Title the graph "Our Brothers and Sisters" and list categories such as "None," "One," "Two," "Three" and "Four." Count with the children how many of them have no brothers or sisters, how many have one brother or sister, etc.

Shape Graph — Title the graph "Our Toys" and list categories such as "Round," "Square," "Triangular" and "Rectangular." Have the children count the number of round toys in the room, the number of square toys, etc.

Pet Graph — Title the graph "Our Pets" and list categories such as "Dogs," "Cats," "Goldfish" and "Hamsters." Count with the children how many of them have dogs, how many have cats, etc.

Food Graph — Title the graph "Our Favorite Foods" and list categories such as "Chicken," "Corn," "Ice Cream" and "Watermelon." Count with the children how many of them like chicken the best, how many like corn the best, etc.

Other Suggestions: Choose topics such as these: colors of hair (brown, black, etc.); numbers of riding toys (trikes, wagons, etc.); kinds of shoes (tie-ons, strap-ons, etc.); favorite stories ("The Three Bears," "Little Red Riding Hood," etc.).

Teaching Graph

47

Teaching Cards

Materials: Large index cards; felt-tip markers.

General Directions: Use index cards to make a set of 12 game cards. On each set of four cards, draw pictures that are alike in some way (a red apple, a red car, a red horn, a red balloon; etc.). To play, lay out three cards containing pictures that are alike and one card containing a picture that is different. Then ask the children to identify the different picture and explain why it doesn't belong with the other three. Continue the game, using combinations of the other cards.

Color Cards — Make four cards containing red pictures, four cards containing yellow pictures and four cards containing blue pictures.

Number Cards — Make four cards containing pictures of one object, four cards containing pictures of two objects and four cards containing pictures of three objects.

Shape Cards — Make four cards containing pictures of round objects (a ball, a clock face, etc.), four cards containing pictures of square objects (a box, an alphabet block, etc.) and four cards containing pictures of triangular objects (a clown hat, a teepee, etc.).

Beginning Sounds Cards — Make four cards containing pictures of things whose names begin with the "b" sound (a bear, a boat, etc.), four cards containing pictures of things whose names begin with the "c" sound (a cat, a cup, etc.) and four cards containing pictures of things whose names begin with the "d" sound (a dog, a doll, etc.).

48

Animal Cards — Make four cards containing pictures of farm
animals (a pig, a cow, etc.), four cards containing pictures of
sea animals (a fish, an octopus, etc.) and four cards containing
pictures of zoo animals (a tiger, an elephant, etc.).

Other Suggestions: Make cards containing pictures of
foods (fruits, vegetables, meats); make cards containing
pictures of vehicles (land, sea, air). Use the cards to play sorting
games (red pictures in one pile, yellow pictures in another pile,
etc.).

Teaching Cards

Teaching Pockets

Materials: A butcher-style apron; assorted colors of felt; pair of scissors; sewing machine or needle and thread; small objects (miniature toys, game parts, crayons, etc.); tagboard; felt-tip marker.

General Directions: Cut four to six large pocket shapes out of different colors of felt and sew them on the apron. Cut shapes, numerals, etc., out of felt and place them on the pockets. Then put on the apron and let the children take turns placing small objects or concept cards into the pockets as you give directions.

Color Pockets — Discuss the apron pocket colors and ask the children to find small matching colored objects around the room. Then have them put the objects into the appropriate pockets.

Number Pockets — Cut different numerals out of felt and place them on the pockets. Then ask the children to put corresponding numbers of small objects into the pockets.

Shape Pockets — Cut different basic shapes (a circle, a square, a triangle, a star, etc.) out of felt and place them on the pockets. Cut matching shapes out of tagboard and ask the children to put them into the appropriate pockets.

Alphabet Pockets — Cut different capital letters out of felt and place them on the pockets. Write corresponding lower case letters on tagboard squares and ask the children to put them into the appropriate pockets.

Beginning Sounds Pockets — Cut different alphabet letters out of felt and place them on the pockets. Provide a collection of small objects whose names begin with those letters and ask the children to put them into the appropriate pockets.

Other Suggestions: Sort small toys (plastic animals, cars and trucks, etc.); sort pictures of foods, clothing, etc. (Make concept cards to place on the pockets by backing pictures with felt strips.)

Teaching Pockets

Teaching Puzzles

Materials: Large index cards; pair of scissors; felt-tip markers.

General Directions: Cut five or six index cards into two-part puzzles. Draw a shape, an alphabet letter, etc., on one part of each puzzle and a matching shape, letter, etc., on the other part. Then mix up the puzzle pieces and let the children take turns finding the match-ups.

Color Puzzles — Draw a different colored circle on one part of each puzzle and a matching colored circle on the other part. Or write a different color word ("Red," "Blue," etc.) on one part of each puzzle and draw a matching colored circle on the other part.

Number Puzzles — Write a different numeral on one part of each puzzle and draw a corresponding number of dots or small pictures on the other part.

Shape Puzzles — Draw a different basic shape (a circle, a square, a triangle, a star, etc.) on one part of each puzzle and a matching shape on the other part.

Alphabet Puzzles — Write a different capital letter on one part of each puzzle and a corresponding lower case letter on the other part.

Beginning Sounds Puzzles — Write a different alphabet letter on one part of each puzzle and draw a picture of something whose name begins with that letter on the other part.

Other Suggestions: Match spelling words with pictures; match patterns (stripes, squiggles, etc.); match pieces of textured materials (velvet, burlap, sandpaper, etc.); match pictures of animals, foods, vehicles, etc.

Teaching Puzzles

Teaching Snacks

Materials: Assorted snacks.

General Directions: Once or twice a week, prepare snacks to reinforce different learning concepts. Discuss the characteristics of each snack at serving time. Then let the children eat while they learn from the special snack you have prepared.

Color Snacks — Choose a color such as red and serve red snack items (strawberries, red gelatin, Cranapple juice, red apple slices, etc.). Use red placemats and napkins, too, if desired.

Number Snacks — Choose a number such as "3" and serve snack items in groups of threes (three raisins, three peanuts, three banana slices, three crackers, etc.).

Shape Snacks — Choose a geometric shape such as a circle and serve round snack items (round crackers, cucumber slices, blueberries, Cheerios, sandwiches cut into rounds, etc.).

Size Snacks — Serve combinations of large and small snack items (sandwiches and raisins, orange segments and shelled peanuts, etc.).

Texture Snacks — Serve combinations of different textured snack items (soft banana slices and crunchy pretzels, creamy yogurt and chewy fruit leather, etc.).

Other Suggestions: Use cookie cutters to cut sandwiches or finger Jell-O into holiday shapes, animal shapes, etc. Serve snacks that tie in with units you are teaching (fry bread for a unit on American Indians, carrot sticks dipped in honey for a unit on bees, etc.). Prepare snacks with the children to teach math and science concepts (weighing and measuring, observing how foods change as they are processed and cooked, etc.).

Teaching Snacks

Teaching Buttons

Materials: An assortment of buttons; muffin tin (optional); large index cards; felt-tip marker.

General Directions: Provide buttons in a variety of colors, shapes, etc. Then let the children use the buttons to play sorting and matching games.

Color Buttons — Have the children sort the buttons by color (use a muffin tin for a holder, if desired). Or lay out several different colored buttons and have the children place matching colored buttons next to them.

Number Buttons — Have the children count the buttons by color, by shape or by size. Or lay out index cards with numerals written on them and have the children place corresponding numbers of buttons on the cards.

Shape Buttons — Have the children sort the buttons by shape (round, square, flower shaped, etc.). Or lay out several different shaped buttons and have the children place matching shaped buttons next to them.

Size Buttons — Have the children sort the buttons by size (large, medium, small). Or lay out several different sized buttons and have the children place matching sized buttons next to them.

Texture Buttons — Have the children sort the buttons by texture or by material. Or lay out several different textured buttons and have the children place matching textured buttons next to them.

Other Suggestions: Sort buttons by number of holes. Use buttons to make math equations (two white buttons plus one black button, etc.). Lay out buttons in patterns (red, blue, red, blue; large, medium, small, large, medium, small; etc.).

Teaching Buttons

Teaching Shapes

Materials: Red, yellow and blue tagboard; pair of scissors.

General Directions: From red tagboard, cut out a large circle, a medium-sized square and a small triangle. From yellow tagboard, cut out a large square, a medium-sized triangle and a small circle. From blue tagboard, cut out a large triangle, a medium-sized circle and a small square. Mix up the shapes and lay them out on a tabletop or on the floor. Then have the children sort the shapes as you give directions. (Note: If desired, make more than one set of shapes out of each color of tagboard.)

Color Shapes — Ask the children to place the red shapes in one pile, the yellow shapes in another pile and the blue shapes in a third pile. Or ask them to lay out the shapes in a pattern (yellow, blue, red, yellow, blue, red, etc.).

Number Shapes — Ask the children to count the shapes by color, by size and by kind of shape. Or ask them to place three shapes next to two shapes, etc., and then tell how many shapes there are all together.

Shape Shapes — Ask the children to place the circles in one pile, the squares in another pile and the triangles in a third pile. Or ask them to lay out the shapes in a pattern (triangle, square, circle, triangle, square, circle, etc.).

Size Shapes — Ask the children to place the large shapes in one pile, the medium-sized shapes in another pile and the small shapes in a third pile. Or ask them to place each set of shapes in a pile with the largest shape on the bottom, the medium-sized shape in the middle and the smallest shape on the top.

Picture Shapes — Let the children put the shapes together on the tabletop or on the floor to make designs or pictures. *add to LP's*

Other Suggestions: Use the shapes as patterns for tracing designs on construction paper. *add to LP's*

Hang on corrugated crdld w/ golf tee poked in.

Teaching Shapes

59

Teaching Cups

Materials: A 6-cup muffin tin; cupcake liners; felt-tip markers; assorted colors of construction paper; pair of scissors; small objects (buttons, beads, pennies, etc.); picture stickers.

General Directions: Draw shapes, numerals, etc., on the bottoms of six cupcake liners and place them in the muffin tin cups. Cut matching shapes out of construction paper or assemble the desired kind and number of small objects. Then let the children sort the shapes or objects into the appropriate muffin tin cups. (Note: An egg carton cut in half can be substituted for the muffin tin and cupcake liners.)

Color Cups — Color the bottom of each cupcake liner a different color. Cut small matching colored circles out of construction paper or provide the children with matching colored buttons or beads.

Number Cups — Number the bottoms of the cupcake liners from 1 to 6 and place them in the muffin tin cups in random order. Provide the children with 21 buttons, beads, etc.

Shape Cups — Draw a different basic shape (a circle, a square, a triangle, a star, etc.) on the bottom of each cupcake liner. Cut small matching shapes out of construction paper.

Picture Cups — Attach a different picture sticker to the bottom of each cupcake liner. Attach matching picture stickers to small construction paper circles.

Classification Cups — Place a different kind of small object in each muffin tin cup (a penny in one cup, a button in another cup, etc.). Provide the children with a box containing a number of each kind of small object.

Other Suggestions: Write capital letters on the bottoms of the cupcake liners and corresponding lower case letters on construction paper circles. Place circles of different patterned wallpaper or wrapping paper in the muffin tin cups and cut out matching patterned circles.

Teaching Cups

Activities, songs and new ideas are waiting for you in each and every issue of the TOTLINE newsletter.

Each issue puts the fun in teaching with 24 pages full of challenging and creative seasonal activities for working with young children — songs and stories, creative art and movement, learning games, science, language, sugarless snack recipes and a special infant and toddler page. You will find the TOTLINE newsletter an indispensable source of fresh new ideas. Page for page, there are more usable activities in the TOTLINE than in any other early childhood education newsletter.

Sample issue $1 • One year subscription $15 (6 issues)

Order from Warren Publishing House, Inc., Dept. B, P.O. Box 2255, Everett, WA 98203

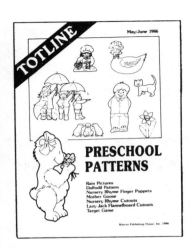

Available from Totline

Super Snacks (64 pg) $3.95

Teaching Tips (64 pg) $3.95

Teaching Toys (64 pg) $3.95

Piggyback Songs (64 pg) $4.95

More Piggyback Songs (96 pg) $6.95

Piggyback Songs for Infants and Toddlers (80 pg) $6.95

Piggyback Songs in Praise of God (80 pg) $6.95

Piggyback Songs in Praise of Jesus (96 pg) $7.95

1-2-3 Art (160 pg) $12.95

1-2-3 Games (80 pg) $6.95

Teeny-Tiny Folktales (80 pg) $6.95

Short-Short Stories (80 pg) $6.95

Mini-Mini Musicals (80 pg) $6.95

"Cut & Tell" Scissor Stories for Fall (80 pg) $5.95

"Cut & Tell" Scissor Stories for Winter (80 pg) $5.95

"Cut & Tell" Scissor Stories for Spring (80 pg) $5.95

Totline Parent Flyers, Book I (128 pg) $14.95

Crafts (80 pg) $7.95

Learning Games (80 pg) $7.95

Language Games (80 pg) $7.95

Story Time (80 pg) $7.95

Movement Time (80 pg) $7.95

Science Time (80 pg) $7.95

Check your local school supply store for these outstanding books or write for our FREE catalog.

Warren Publishing House, Inc.
P.O. Box 2255, Dept. B
Everett, WA 98203